Jewels of North East

A Travel Guide

By Sarah Lee

Jewels of North East England Copyright 2013 by Sarah Lee

All rights reserved. No part of this publication may be reproduced, distributed, or transmitted in any form or by any means, including photocopying, recording, or other electronic or mechanical methods, without the prior written permission of the publisher, except in the case of brief quotations embodied in critical reviews and certain other non-commercial uses permitted by copyright law

Contents

Introduction 5
Newcastle Upon Tyne 7
China Town 唐人街 10
Theatre and Music Venues 11
The Laing Art Gallery 13
Shopping in Newcastle 14
Evening Entertainment in Newcastle 16
The Sage 19
Whitley Bay 21
Tynemouth 22
Tynemouth Castle and Priory 24
Seaton Sluice 26
South Shields 27
Marsden Rock 29
Bede's World 32
Washington Old Hall 37
Durham 39
Durham Castle 43

Durham Cathedral	46
Beamish	49
Finchale Abbey	53
High Force	54
Barnard Castle	56
The Bowes Museum	57
Penshaw Monument	58
Alnwick Castle	60
Bamburgh	62
The Grace Darling Museum	64
St Aidan's Church	67
Holy Island	69
The Farne Islands	75
Inner Farne Island	77
Longstone Island	79
Chester Le Street	101
Raby Castle	104
More Books By Sarah Lee	107
Addresses of Attractions	112

Introduction

North East England with its beautiful coastlines and historic buildings is popular among tourists far and wide. I wanted to create a guide of places I know and love and wanted to show you whether you are local or visitors the crown jewels of the North east.

Over the last 2000 years, The Romans, Anglo Saxons, Vikings, Normans, Tudors and Victorians have all left their mark on the landscape, enabling us to take a step back in time and discover our roots in this country.

Every place has its own charm, whether it be natural beauty or importance historically, they are places I recommend you visit if you come to the North East. This guide can be used time and time again, to remind you of great days out the North East has to offer, or can be used as a travel guide so you can plan your day to day travels whilst you visit the North East. It can also be used as a token of memorabilia after your trip.

Even if you just find yourself here on a business trip, you may want to use this guide to see some of the sights before you return home.

Most of the attractions mentioned in the book are open from Easter Weekend, until the Winter season. Most of them close for the Winter but I have included post codes and telephones numbers of the places to help you plan your trip.

Some of the sights such as Holy Island and St Mary's Lighthouse, have a causeway that is open depending on the tides, so it is important you prepare in advance of your trip.

I hope you enjoy your visit to the North East, and hope this guide is of use to you. It has been a pleasure to create.

Newcastle Upon Tyne

Newcastle Upon Tyne is a vibrant city that has roots dating back to AD122 when it grew from the Roman Settlement of Pons Aelius. Famous for its seven bridges across the River Tyne including the Millennium Eye, its large shopping centre and its lively nightlife, it attracts visitors from far and wide. Visit the popular Eldon Square shopping centre on Northumberland Street, or explore the Quayside .

Newcastle Castle Keep

The site of the Castle Keep was the site of a Roman Fort and was used to guard Hadrian's Wall. Later it was used as a Saxon cemetery from the 7th century until the castle was constructed in 1080. The new castle that was built gave the town its name and is now a grade 1 listed building. It was founded by the eldest son of William the Conqueror. By the fourteenth century the town was fortified with a wall that had six main gates. The Keep was used as a prison for the County of Northumberland until the civil war broke out in 1642 and was once again used as a fortified stronghold. Today Visitors can explore the Castle Keep which provides remarkable views of the surrounding area and seven bridges from its rooftop.

The Black Gate

The fortified gatehouse was originally the entrance to Newcastle. It was built between 1247 and 1250. The medieval guard rooms on either side of the vaulted passageway still exist today. Look for the slits they used for their crossbows. The sills were angled to allow them to fire down into the ditch. .

China Town 唐人街

Popular with the Asian community and locals, Stowell Street in Newcastle is the place to eat if you like oriental food. It is positioned near St James Park, and comes alive at night. Just walking down the street will make you feel you are in the far east. It is also the place where the Asian community celebrate Chinese New Year, and put on an elaborate street display for anyone who cares to watch.

Theatre and Music Venues

The Theatre Royal (Above) is famous for its entertainment. Open since 1837, and a grade 1 listed building, the theatre provides top entertainment in drama, dance music and comedy and situated in the heart of Newcastle City Centre.

The Empire Theatre in Sunderland is almost on a par with the Theatre Royal in the type of shows it provides and is situated in Sunderland City Centre.

The O2 Academy is a newly refurbished venue for new and upcoming artists and bands.

The City Hall in Newcastle is also a popular venue for artists new and old, and the Metro Radio Arena is a large music venue for the biggest names in the music Industry.

The Laing Art Gallery

Visit the Laing Art Gallery in the centre of the City Centre for free. It has a large collection of oil and water colours including works by the famous artist JMW Turner and others. The Gallery has programme of free events which include gallery talks, family activities and artists' events.

The permanent collection of art is displayed throughout the season with paintings by John Martin, William Holman-Hunt, Sir Lawrence Alma-Tadema and sculpture by Henry Moore, amongst others.

Shopping in Newcastle

Eldon Square is in the centre of Newcastle City Centre and has a wide selection of shops and restaurants.

The Metro Centre in Gateshead.

The Metro Centre is a 10 minute drive from Newcastle City Centre. It is a large indoor shopping centre with over 340 shops and is currently the largest indoor shopping centre in the UK. It is the site of the new Odeon Cinema complex. Its red, green, yellow, and blue zones all have their own free car park. And the centre is open until 9pm weekdays, 7pm on Saturdays and 5pm on Sundays. Inside there is always fun things for kids to do, including an amusement arcade, with dodgem cars, bungy jumping, a train ride that trundles through the shopping centre, and an indoor theatre is a regular occurrence. There is a wide variety of eating places near the cinema, and a food village.

There is a bus service that leaves from Newcastle City Centre Bus Station, stand E bus no 47, the journey is twenty minutes to Gateshead Metro Centre.

Evening Entertainment in Newcastle
The Gate

The Gate in Newcastle is popular and is full of bars and restaurants and has an Empire cinema and Aspers Casino inside.

The Aspers Sports Bar below with its huge 138" multimedia wall is a popular gathering place to watch the latest sports events.

16

Clubs, there are many. Tiger Tiger next door to The Gate, is popular, as it has many different themed bars, nightclub. and a restaurant in one building. Revolution, The Riverside at the Quayside, and Bambu in the town centre are popular.

The Hyena Comedy Club nearby is a popular venue, open until 2am, it is a bar, restaurant that provides comedy entertainment from known and up coming comedians.

The Quayside

The quayside is the upmarket place to dine and go clubbing but can be expensive. The Pitcher and Piano affords brilliant views of the River and Bridges, and is one of the most expensive bars in the area. The Cooperage bar is popular with Salsa dancers and has Salsa music most days. The Chase is a popular bar, as is Jimmyz.

The Bigg Market

The Bigg market can get very loud, as it is full of bars and restaurants and popular with local revellers. Bars near Newcastle Central Train Station are also becoming more popular. The Lodge, partly owned by Ant and Dec is a winner with the locals.

The Sage

The Sage is a state of the art music venue and conference centre. It has two halls one for 1600 people the other for 600 people. It is a stunning piece of architecture that sits on the river bank opposite Newcastle Quayside.

Inside is just as stunning, with its curvy walls and lights, and the acoustics in the building are first class. Inside you will also find a superb café, brasserie and four bars and it offers amazing views of the quayside, river and bridges.

Inside The Sage

Whitley Bay

Whitley Bay is a popular North East seaside town. Its main feature is the enchanting St Mary's Lighthouse shown above. It is accessible via a causeway when the tide is out and visitors can climb the 137 steps to the top of the lighthouse to gain spectacular views of the coastline. It is popular with the local children as its rockpools provide a fantastic opportunity for the children to explore. To get the best out of your trip it is best to contact the lighthouse prior to travelling to find out the tide timetable and its opening times as they vary according to the tide.

Tynemouth

  Tynemouth is a picturesque seaside town in North East England. Its Castle and Priory occupy the headland, but it is also a place of long white sandy beaches and interesting landscapes. Head to Tynemouth if you enjoy an area steeped in history, and want to explore the historic Castle and Priory, or you can visit the popular Blue Reef Aquarium, or spend time relaxing on the white sandy beaches or walking along the beautiful coast line.

King Edwards Bay Tynemouth

The Blue Reef Aquarium at Tynemouth has many natural themed habitats and a wide variety of sea creatures and now an Amassonian themed habitat where you can view a colony of monkeys. There are many large viewing areas including an underwater tunnel which provides excellent views of the fish above.

Tynemouth Castle and Priory

The headland at Tynemouth is steeped in history and natural beauty. On arriving at the entrance to the castle you can't help but admire the beauty of the fortified gatehouse and the colour of the stone. It stands majestic on the cliff top, high above the white sanded beaches below. It is surrounded by the sea and to the front a deep ditch. You can appreciate how it has survived for over 600 years. For a small fee you can roam around and explore the castle gatehouse and priory. A spiral staircase in the gatehouse will lead you to the top offering splendid views of the surroundings. You can even see Penshaw Monument fourteen miles away from this vantage point.

Signs of war are evident. The priory itself has roots back to the 8th century, where a wooden monastery existed, but this was destroyed during the Viking raids. The priory was formed in the 11th century. St Oswine's remains were held there in a shrine up until 1539. Henry the V111 , after charging the monks with serious misconduct, took over the monastery, and is responsible for the taking of the gold and silver, breaking up St Oswine's shrine, and scattering his bones. Henry made the site into a fortress and it was used to defend the entrance to the Tyne. The gun platforms were installed and were in use up until 1956, and were manned during many wars including the Napoleonic wars and first and second world wars.

Seaton Sluice

A few miles north of Whitley Bay is the charming coastline fishing village of Seaton Sluice. The small boats in the harbour and the white sandy beaches make it popular with locals and tourists alike.

South Shields

South Shields is a popular seaside town with tourists and locals as it provides many of the traditional features expected of a seaside town in a concentrated area. Souter Lighthouse is an iconic landmark in South Shields. Visitors can enjoy climbing the 76 steps to the top for a superb view of the coastline and surroundings. They can also experience what life was like for the Lighthouse Keeper, with a reconstructed Victorian Keepers cottage.

South Shields has wide award winning sandy beaches, a fun fairground, the Ocean Beach Pleasure Park, that has rides to suit all ages. It has amusements, a large park with boating facilities, a pirate themed mini adventure golf, Smugglers Cove, a large shopping centre, museums, and a large selections of cafes, restaurants and pubs. South Shields is also home to other famous tourist sites including Bede's World, Arbeia Roman Fort and Marsden Grotto.

Marsden Rock

Marsden Rock and beach.

Marsden Rock, is a 100 foot Magnesian Limestone rock that is home to nesting cormorants, kittiwakes and fulmars. It was once famous for its natural archway but the rock collapsed during a severe winter in 1996/1997 causing the rock to split in two.

Marsden Grotto is a pub and restaurant that is built inside a cave. It is unique as it is the only cave restaurant in Europe. It has a two hundred year history and has been linked to pirates and smugglers in the past. It is decorated with pirate figures, fishing nets, and skulls to help visitors appreciate the area's history as a pirate dwelling. There is a lift from the cliff top that takes you down to the restaurant and bar and allows access to the beach below. Access to the beach can also be made via the modern stairwell from the cliff top.

Marsden Grotto above.

Arbeia Roman Fort

Arbeia is a reconstruction on the site of the original fort built by the Romans around 160 AD whom occupied it until the 5th century. The fort was then used to guard the entrance into the River Tyne and provided military supplies to the forts positioned along Hadrian's Wall. The Roman gatehouse and barracks have been reconstructed on their original foundations. You can gain a unique insight into the life of the Roman soldiers of that time by visiting the reconstructions of the West Gate, the Commanding Officer's House and Barrack Block viewing the displays within.

The site is still a live archaeological site and more discoveries are made each day. Evidence of their excavations are on view in the museum. . There are often live mock battles at the site please contact the fort for further information.

Bede's World

Bede's World is a museum attributed to The Venerable Bede. St Bede lived in the monastery in Jarrow in the 7th century and due to his writings we are able to gain an accurate insight into life at that time. The museum itself has on display artefacts excavated on the monastic site and displays of how the monks would have lived during Anglo Saxon times.

The architecture is in keeping with the Anglo Saxon buildings and the Roman influence around at that time. Outside you can walk around the Roman terrace, and explore the Anglo Saxon farm which has herbs, vegetables and breed of animals that were typical of the time of Bede. The monks during Bede's time would have farmed the land and cared for the farm animals as well as diligently prepared manuscripts such as the Codex Amiatinus one of the oldest bible manuscripts.

A short walk away is St Paul's Church. Parts of it date back to the 7th century and inside you can find the original stone slab dating back to 685 AD.

St Paul's church has been a place of pilgrimage for over 1300 years. It was the site of the twin monastery where the Venerable Bede started his life as a monk from the tender age of 7 years. He devoted his life to God and to study and his works are used internationally today. His most famous work is *Historia ecclesiastica gentis Anglorum* (The Ecclesiastical History of the English People), and gained him the title of 'The father of English History.'

St Paul's Church dates back to 681 and some of the original stonework is still incorporated within the church building. The three small chancel windows are Anglo-Saxon and originally contained coloured glass.

Inside the church you can view the original stone slab which is inscribed with a Latin inscription, the dedication of the church on 23 April AD 685.

DEDICATIO BASILICAE
SCI PAUL VIIII KL MAI
ANNO XV EFRIDI REG
CEOLFRIDI ABB EIUSDEM
Q ECCLES DO AVCTORE
CONDITORIS ANNO IIII

This translates as: 'The dedication of the basilica of St. Paul on the 9th day before the Kalens of May in the 15th year of King Ecgfrith and in the fourth year of Abbot Ceolfrith founder, by God's guidance, of the same church.'

Bede's World will transport you back in time to the time of Bede and the English roots of the Anglo-Saxon period of the 7th century and allows you to explore the full sized Anglo-Saxon buildings. Viewing life in that time , seeing how our ancestors lived, the materials they used to build houses, how they worked the land, the animals they kept and the herbs and vegetables they grew is truly an inspiring educational experience for all ages.

Washington Old Hall

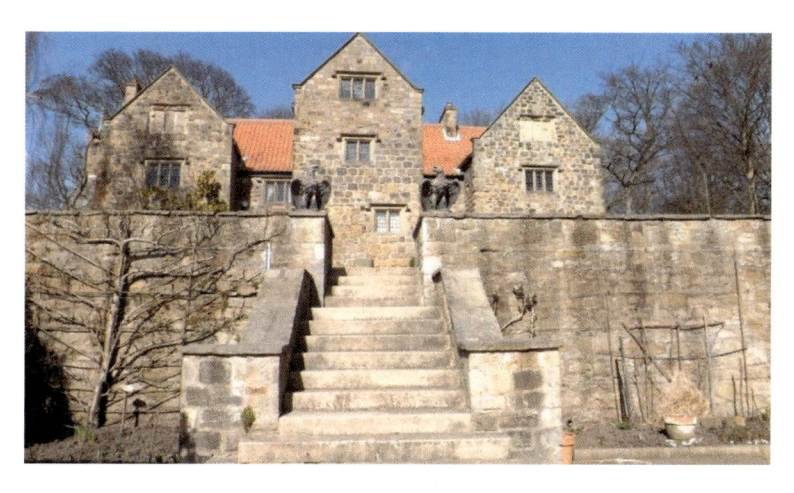

Washington Old Hall has become famous as it is the home of the ancestors of George Washington, commander-in-chief of the Continental Army during the American Revolutionary War and who became the first president of the United States of America in 1788. The capital city of America was named Washington after their first president, his name originated from Washington Old Hall in Washington, in North East England. The interior of the manor has changed many times over the centuries, and is now typical of a 17th century manor. Inside you will find memorabilia displayed of George Washington including portraits given by benefactors during the Hall's restoration.

Visitors from America come here interested in George Washington's roots and they hold a special independence day ceremony every 4th July.

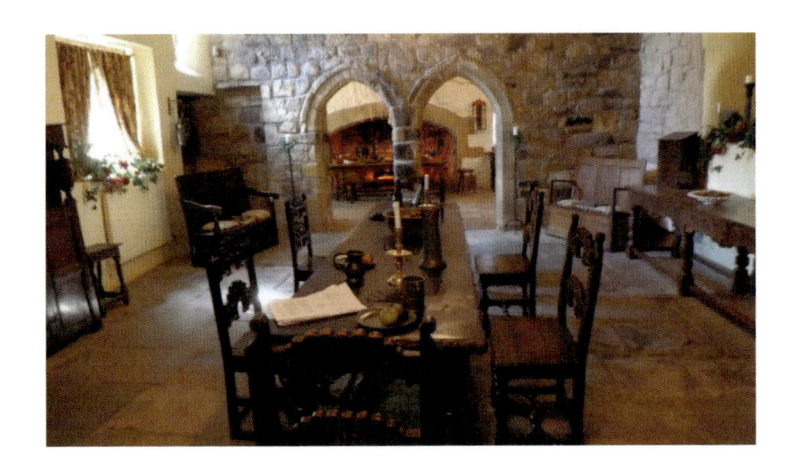

Durham

Durham was the place chosen to bury the remains of St Cuthbert . The monks were looking for a burial place and St Cuthbert had appeared to them in a dream and they believed Durham was the place he was guiding them to. The Cathedral and Castle were built on the peninsula surrounded by the River Wear, and the city grew from there.

The river, with its tranquillity and beauty draws visitors to its banks. There are opportunities for rowing or taking a pleasure trip along the river.

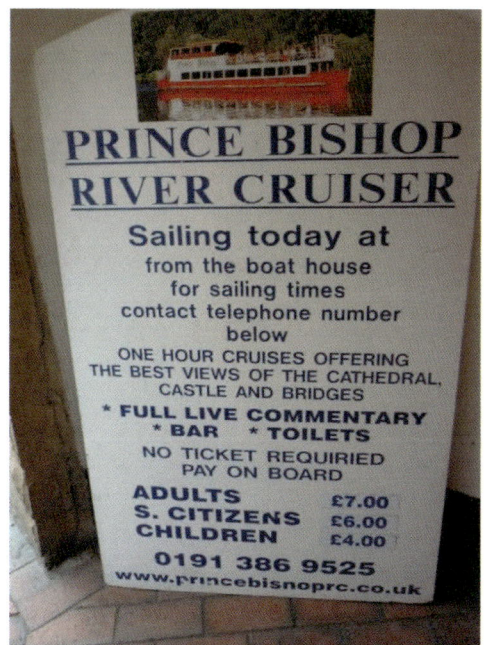

PRINCE BISHOP RIVER CRUISER

Sailing today at
from the boat house
for sailing times
contact telephone number
below

ONE HOUR CRUISES OFFERING
THE BEST VIEWS OF THE CATHEDRAL,
CASTLE AND BRIDGES

* FULL LIVE COMMENTARY
* BAR   * TOILETS

NO TICKET REQUIRIED
PAY ON BOARD

ADULTS   £7.00
S. CITIZENS   £6.00
CHILDREN   £4.00

0191 386 9525
www.princebisnoprc.co.uk

Durham has a small city centre with a wide selection of shops and restaurants. Durham is a market town with a large indoor market. The shops surround the charming square which provides a relaxed cosy ambience.

Durham Castle

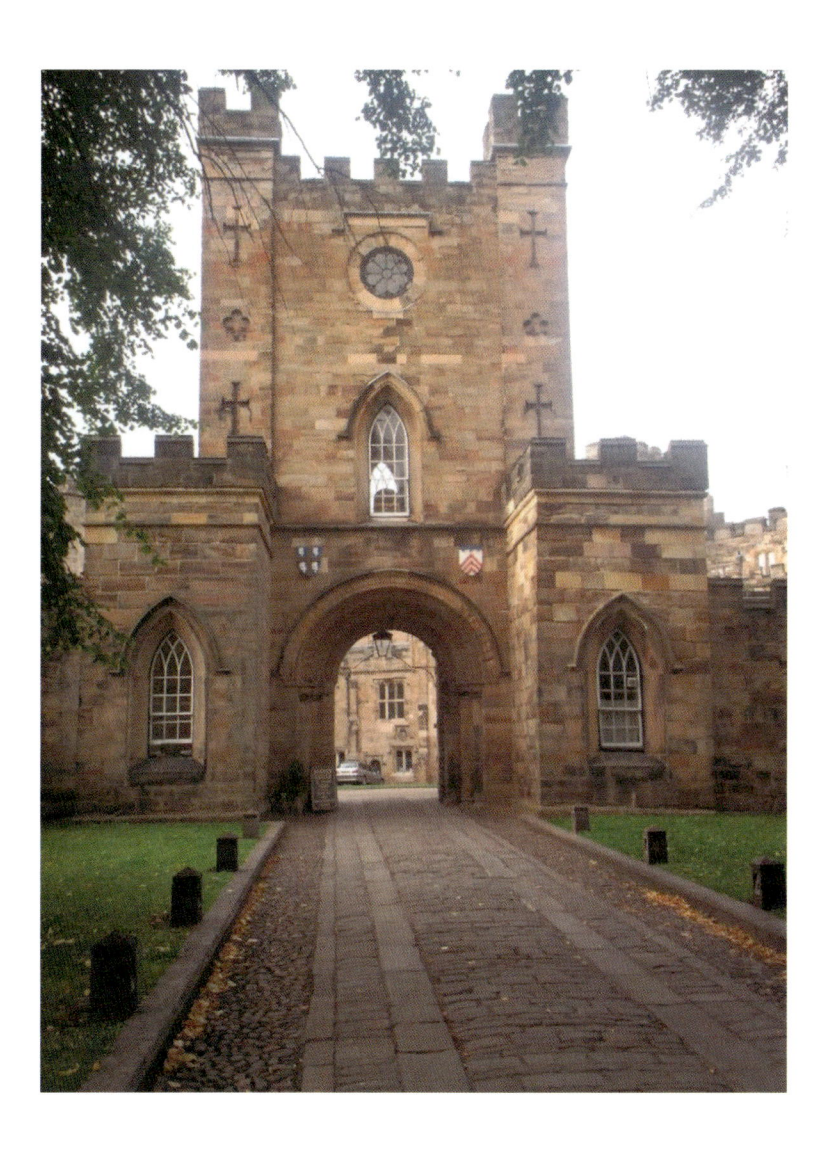

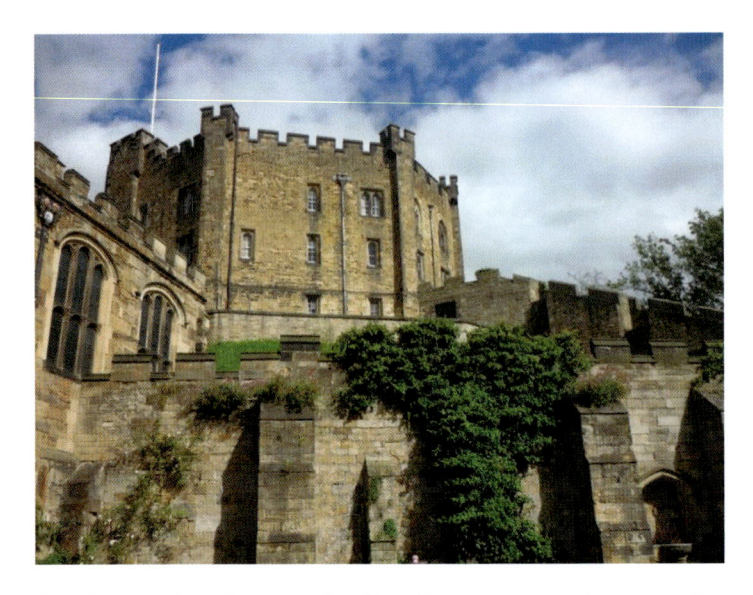

Durham Castle was built almost one thousand years ago during Norman times and was originally a fortress on a manufactured hill. Durham is unique in that it was controlled by the Prince Bishops. The Prince Bishops had control over the castle and lived there for a time. They were powerful men given secular powers by the King, and controlled armies and the law courts.

The castle is now home to around eighty university students and some of the rooms are let to paying guests. The building has changed constantly over the centuries but there is still the original stonework evident in the chapel dating back to the 11th century.

The castle is open all year round, but visits are restricted to paying for the guided tour only. The ticket for the tour is via the library adjacent to the castle. I found the tour guide humorous and informative and was well worth the small fee. The tour lasts around 45 minutes. The only downside is there is no gift shop in the castle but there are trinkets available to buy at the library.

Durham Cathedral

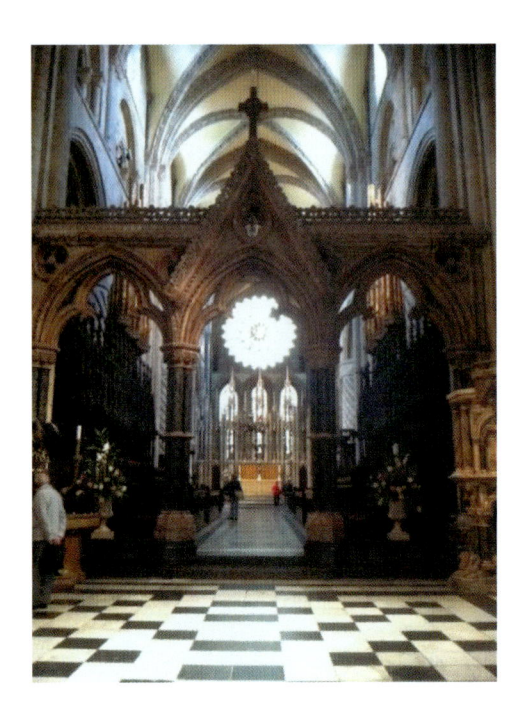

On entering the cathedral you will be greeted by the stern face of the sanctuary knocker.

It represents the right of sanctuary that was once offered to fugitives who were unarmed. They would be served food and drink but would be asked to wear a yellow cross of St Cuthbert on their left shoulder. There were 331 fugitives between 1464 and 1525, 283 were murderers. The knocker on the door is a replica of the original that can be found in the Treasures of St Cuthbert exhibition.

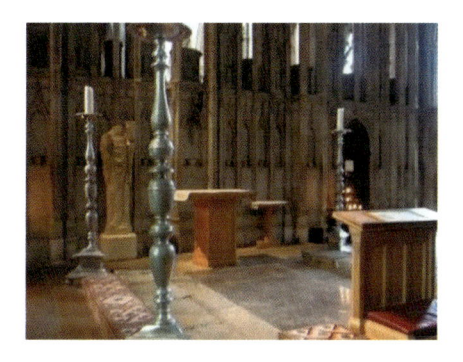

St Cuthbert is considered the greatest saint of the north. He died in 687 after living as a monk then a Bishop. His tomb lies behind the alter and as his resting place has been associated with miraculous healings since his death, pilgrims still flock to his burial place today. You can visit 'The Treasures of St Cuthbert exhibition inside the Cathedral, but their is a fee for this.

St Bede is also interred at Durham Cathedral.

The Cathedral stands on the other side of the green to the Castle, both are just a short walk from the city centre. There is a large gift shop and a restaurant inside the cathedral. Visitors are expected to pay on entry.

Beamish

Beamish is a living open air museum that brings the past back to life. It incorporates a small village and surrounding countryside that aims to give visitors a taste of what life was like for people living in Northern England in the 1930's and 1940's. The whole village is a museum. Visitors can walk around the inside of the houses, looking like the contents have been untouched for 80 years, the shops are as they were then, and visitors can even buy things such as sweets in the stores. The people working there are all in period costumes and work away happily at their tasks, such as baking bread, or making mats.

As the site is so large trams are used to ferry visitors around the site which is a novelty in itself. It is a multi award winning museum including winning awards for the best European museum of the year and the best British Museum of the year and I can say I believe they deserve them. It needs a full day to appreciate the museum and everything it has to offer so please plan your visit wisely. There is an admission charge, but once paid you are free to take as many tram rides as you wish and visit as many places as often as you wish, and I believe at the moment they have an offer where once you have bought a ticket you can go as many times as you wish in a year at no extra charge.

The Dentist's house includes the room where he used to extract teeth and the typical tools of the trade that were used then are on display. On this occasion a man in costume explains the role of the dentist during that time period to the visitors nearby.

The Nursery in the Dentists House.

The school building is a popular place, not only with visitors from far and wide but also local schools come here on educational visits and are encouraged to arrive in period costume where they can sample life as a school child during that time.

As Beamish is such a big site with many houses and buildings to visit, it is advisable to spend the whole day there. If you arrive late in the afternoon you will see very little of the site.

Finchale Abbey

Finchale Abbey was the place St Godric was led to after a vision. Here he lived as a hermit until his death aged 105 years. The Abbey has been used as a holiday retreat by the monks from Durham. The priory building actually dates back to 1115 AD.

It is set in tranquil surroundings near the river and it is easy to see why the monks chose to holiday here. Visitors can walk across the bridge and walk along a beautiful scenic riverside path of the riverside country park and can picnic on the banks, or can explore the ruins of the Abbey itself. There is also an adult only caravan park that overlooks the priory and is popular with tourists looking for a peaceful holiday.

High Force

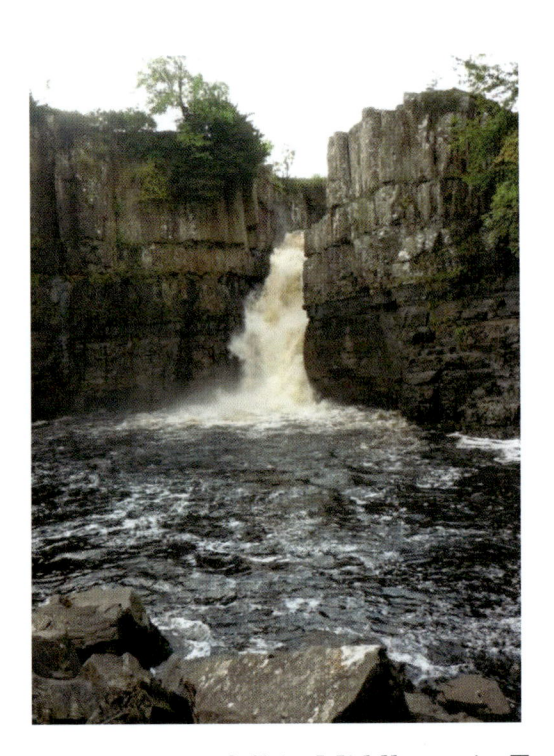

High Force is a waterfall in Middleton in Teesdale where visitors are able to witness the River Tees cascading over the hard igneous rock 20 metres above.

There is a car park across the road from the entrance to the site and for a very small fee visitors are able to access the waterfall via a maintained footpath, through the forest down to the river below. The walkway itself is quite breathtaking, and as you near the waterfall, you can hear its roar before you are able to view it in its entirety.

Barnard Castle

Barnard Castle is a town taking its name from the 12th Century Castle that graces the edge of the town and the River Tees, 20 miles south west of Durham City. It is a popular tourist destination. Close by is the High Force waterfall and the Bowes Museum.

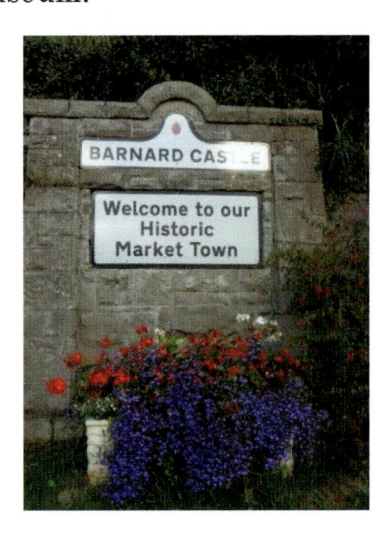

The Bowes Museum

The Bowes Museum, founded by John and Josephine Bowes in the 19th century is a huge display of art, over three floors, that encompasses paintings, ceramics, sculptures and textiles. There is a fashion and textile gallery, displaying artefacts from 1550 to 1970. A ceramics gallery, silver and metals gallery, and exhibitions that vary, as well as a huge collection of stunning paintings.

Penshaw Monument

Penshaw Monument stands 136 metres above sea level on the summit of Penshaw Hill. It can be seen from many miles around and is a popular landmark. It was built as a replica of the Greek Temple Theseion, the Temple of Hephaestus, in Athens. It was built in 1844 in the honour of John George Lambton. The foundation stone was laid by Thomas, Earl of Zetland in front of a crowd containing hundreds of Members of the Provincial Grand Lodges of Freemasons. Visitors can walk up the many steps to the site, and will be rewarded with spectacular views of the surrounding area.

Penshaw Hill is also rumoured to be the setting of the famous story of the Lambton Worm.

The Angel of The North

The Angel of the North was commissioned by Gateshead Council and created by award winning sculptor Antony Gormley. I believe it is currently the world's largest angel sculpture and the most viewed art in the world as it is seen by 90,000 motorists a day that pass it along the A1 making a total of 33 million views of the sculpture each year. It was created in 1997 and was erected at the site in 1998. It stands 20 metres high with a wing span of 54 metres and weighs 200 tonnes. The sculpture is anchored to hundreds of tonnes of concrete 20 metres below the surface and is built to withstand winds of more than 100 mph.

Visitors have free access to the angel and can park their car nearby and walk around the site freely.

Alnwick Castle

Alnwick Castle is the second largest inhabited castle in England, it is home to the Duke and Duchess of Northumberland. Extremely popular with visitors, having nearly a million visitors a year, the castle is not only a building that earns your respect, it is a venue of entertaining activities for the young and old; Made famous by the fact it was a set in the Harry Potter movies, known fondly as Hogwarts. The castle attracts visitors far and wide. After you have explored the exterior and interior grandiose staterooms, you can entertain yourself such as trying your hand at archery, or scaring yourself by visiting the Lost Cellars, or you can practise medieval crafts such as wand making or broomstick training.

There is a courtyard cafe, and a large gift shop. There is also a large treehouse than can be explored walking along rope bridges and inside is a superb unique restaurant.

At an extra cost you can visit the gardens which have cascading water displays and labyrinths.

Bamburgh

Bamburgh is a quaint historic town that is watched over by the majestic Bamburgh Castle that stands proud on top of a basalt outcrop. Bamburgh was chosen by the 6th century Nothumbrian Kings as its capital due to its formidable position high above the coastline. The first timbers of the stockade were laid by the first Anglo Saxon King of Bernicia, Ida the Flamebearer. Historic Bamburgh castle has been associated with powerful men of old, including King Oswald, William the Conqueror and Henry VIII to name but a few.

Bamburgh was also the place where Grace Darling was born and died, and the cemetery in St Aidan's church is her resting place. It is also home to their local heroin's museum The Grace Darling Museum. The castle allows panoramic views of the coastline and the Farne Islands and its interiors will amuse you for hours. It also boasts its own coffee shop serving hot and cold food.

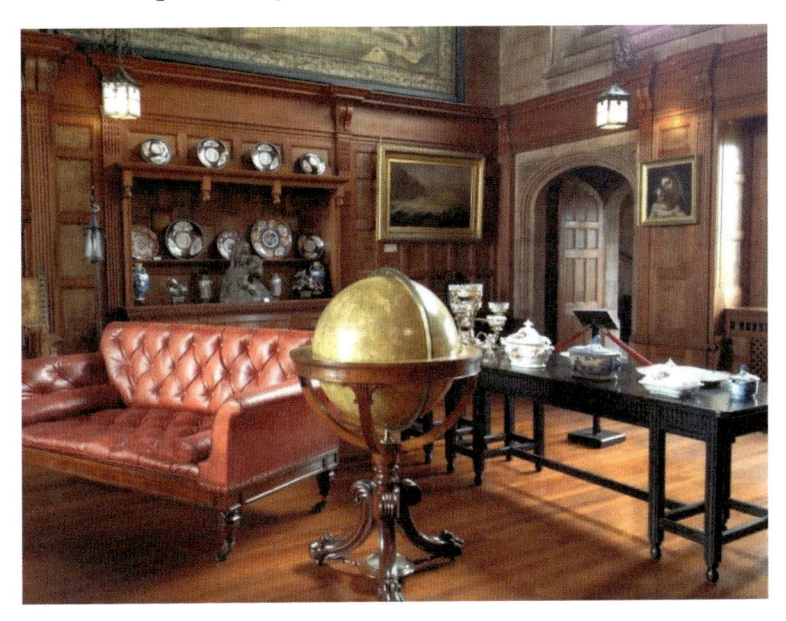

The Grace Darling Museum

Grace Darling became a hero after rowing out in stormy seas and helping her father save the lives of nine men whose ship had been cut in two by the ragged rocks their family lighthouse was warning them of. She died not long after, succumbing to the deadly disease of TB and her memorial stands proud in the graveyard of St Aidan's church opposite the museum.

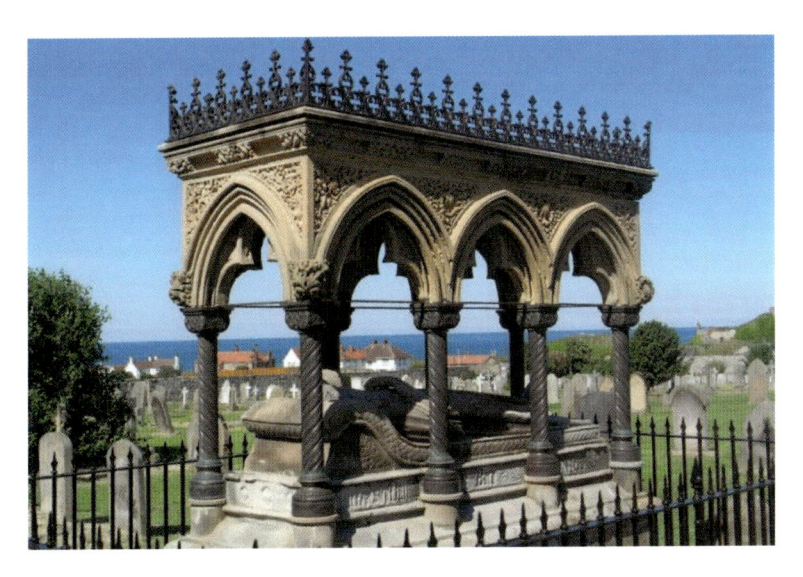

The museum tells her story, in audio, and through pictures and memorabilia and includes many original artefacts associated with the heroin, including the rowing boat used to save the lives of the sailors. It is free entry and there is a gift shop inside.

Above is the house where Grace was born. Just a few yards up the street from the Grace Darling Museum on Radcliffe Road. Above the door is a plaque to mark the event.

Below is The Pantry. It was the house that used to belong to Thomasin her sister, where she ran her dressmaking business. This is the house where grace died on 13 Front Street in Bamburgh.

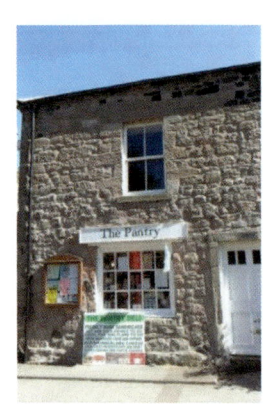

St Aidan's Church

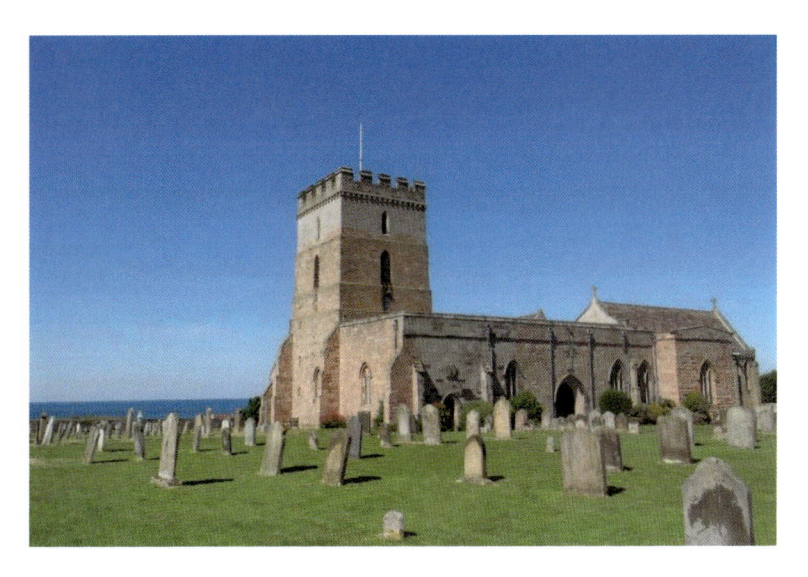

Aidan was an Irish monk who established the Monastery at Lindisfarne, and in 635 built the first church on the request of King Oswald. This church is understood to be on the site of where St Aidan's Church in Bamburgh now stands. On 31st August 651 Aidan was visiting the then parish church, and he was given a tent to sleep in at the side of the church. He was undertaken with a sudden illness and died here with his head against the post that served as a buttress. Even though the church was burnt down twice after then, the buttress remained and some believe it to be miraculous. Much of his biography was written by St Bede.

There is a memorial inside the church to St Aidan at the spot where he died. The church doors are usually open for you to explore the interior.

As the church works closely with the Grace Darling Museum, you will also find a stone carved memorial to Grace Darling inside the church. Grace and her family are buried in the grounds, and there is also a large memorial to Grace in the graveyard.and a stained glass window in her memory.

Holy Island

This tiny island off the north east coast of England was once called Lindisfarne but later named Holy Island because of its ancient past as the sanctimonious retreat of Saint Cuthbert and Saint Aiden. It housed a monastery from AD 634. Saint Aiden was chosen by the king of Northumbria, Oswald to be the Bishop of the monastery and he was successful in establishing the Christian community King Oswald wanted. Aidan spread the Christian word and evangelised the whole of Northumbria.

Saint Cuthbert, the north's most popular saint also became a Bishop of Lindisfarne. The island became and still is a place of pilgrimage because of the Island's history and due to the miracles that had happened after the opening of Saint Cuthbert's coffin eleven years after his death. His body was found to be undecayed and still smelling sweet. People claimed to be cured of illnesses such as tumours, paralysis and the plague after they had prayed near where his body lay.

Lindisfarne Castle

The most outstanding feature of the Island seen from the mainland and many miles away and sits on top of a volcanic mound known as Beblowe Craig is Lindisfarne Castle. For a small fee visitors can explore the castle and its ancient interior and can imagine themselves back in the time it was built in 1550.

The Castle looks amazing both inside and out. The steep pathway to the castle is cobbled, so be sure to wear sensible shoes. There are amazing views from the castle across the Island and beyond, it is well worth a visit. Opening times vary depending on the tides so it paramount to check tidal times before you arrive.

Lindisfarne priory was built in the 12th century on the site of the original monastery of St Cuthbert. You can explore its ruins today for a small fee.

It is the place of inspiration for the Lindisfarne Gospels and has been attacked and pillaged by the Vikings. Events such as mock Viking attacks are held here. Further information can be found on the English Heritage Site.

http://www.english-heritage.org.uk/

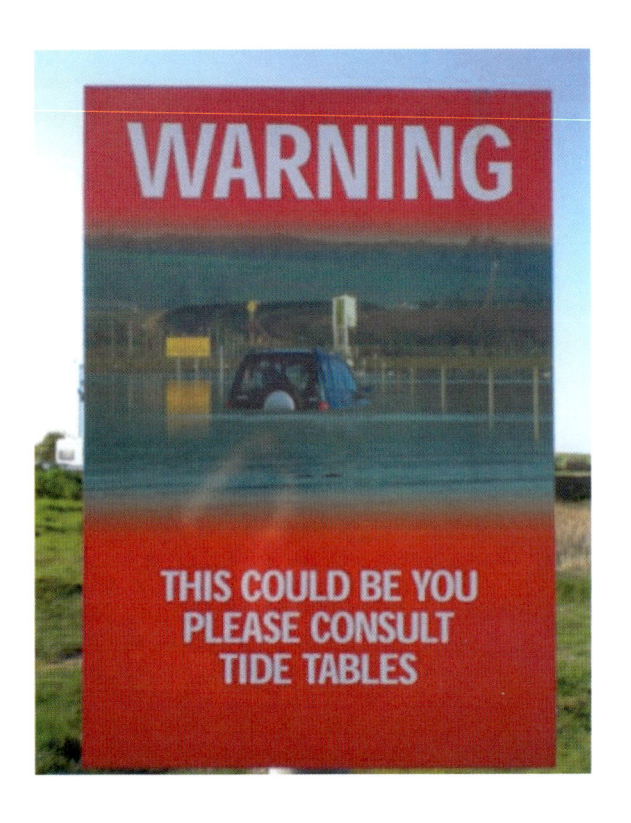

Holy Island is a tidal Island. Opening times for the castle, priory and Lindisfarne centre vary and depend on the tide and crossing times. Its always best to check the opening times before you travel. For opening times and information you can call the National Trust on 01289 389 244 So always plan your journey in advance. The Holy Island crossing times are widely available online or you can ring Northumberland council on Tel: 0845 600 6400.

The Farne Islands

The Farne island is accessible via the North Sunderland Harbour boat trips in the town of Seahouses. It has a fishing port, which is very busy in the summer months as many tourists and visitors come here to explore the Farne Islands. There are several companies that offer boat trips here, some take you around all of the Farne Islands, some also take you on a landing trip to Inner Farne, the hermit home of St Cuthbert in the 7th Century. Some boat trips take you to view the wildlife such as the whales and dolphins, and the many grey seals that live around these Islands. One company takes you to the home of Grace Darling Longstone Island and Lighthouse.

The Kiosks at the the harbour allow you to purchase tickets on the day.

The Farne Islands are also a haven for bird watchers as they are populated with Puffins, Cormorants and Eider Ducks particularly in the breeding season.

Inner Farne Island

Inner Farne was the home of St Cuthbert in the 7th century. He lived here as a hermit for around ten years and died here in the house he built. Today it is the home of the National Trust. Their employees live in the old monastery building Prior Castell's Tower, and monitor the wildlife, catching birds and tagging them. There is also a lighthouse that blinks 24 hours a day, due to the rocky coastline and previous shipwrecks of which the area is littered, making it a popular place for divers. You can visit St Cuthbert's Chapel here, and walk around getting a 360 degree view of the wildlife and surrounding islands and coastline. During your trip around the Islands you will see Longstone Lighthouse, the home of the famous heroin Grace Darling.

Prior Castell's Tower and St Cuthbert's Chapel.

Inside the chapel is a memorial to Grace Darling.

Longstone Island

Longstone Lighthouse was lit on 15th February 1826. Originally manned by a lighthouse keeper, today it is controlled by computers.

Grace Darling lived here until her death in 1842. Her father William was the Lighthouse keeper here until he retired. On 7th September 1838 the Forfarshire paddle steam ship crashed into the rocks about a mile south of the island. Grace spotted the wreckage at 4.45 am with the aid of her telescope, and she spotted survivors clinging tot he rocks. She persuaded her father to go with her in a rowing boat and rescue the people trapped. It was a dangerous mission in the stormy seas, but they managed to save nine lives. Sadly forty three lives were lost. As Grace was a young woman aged only 22 yrs, to risk her life rowing in the stormy seas, she became famous, and became a heroine. The

Duke of Northumberland became her guardian to protect her from much of the unwanted attention that was thrown at her. She was awarded gold and silver medals for her bravery. Sadly she died just a few years later succumbing to the deadly disease of TB. She died in her sister's house in Bamburgh.

The rocks around here are still very hazardous, and ships are still wrecked in this area today. Many lives have been lost here.

One company offers trips to the Island and Lighthouse. The Golden Gate. You can purchase a ticket at the kiosk at North Sunderland Harbour. The trip lasts around 2 hours and for a few extra pounds can go inside the lighthouse for a guided tours. There are a hundred steps to the lantern at the top. But if your health isn't as good you can take a rest in one of the rooms on your way up, or decide not to go to the top and just look at the view from one of the rooms instead.

Some cabinets remain inside the circular lighthouse. They are curved and were specially made to fit the circular rooms and will probably be of no use anywhere else. The rooms are very small, it's hard to imagine how a large family like the Darlings lived here, and as you go up the rooms got smaller. The only storage was a cupboard under the stairs.

The view from the top. You can see Brownsman Island and the Big Harker Rock where the Forfarshire was wrecked from here. The same view Grace would have experienced when she spotted the wreck in 1838.

You will also get to see the amazing lantern that still works today. The light is magnified by the glass prisms, and reaches over 20 miles out to sea. Originally it flashed every 30 seconds, today it flashes every twenty seconds. The lighthouse though does not have lighthouse keepers anymore but is manned by computers.

Above, the lantern in Longstone Lighthouse.

Above Brownsman Island.

Grace Darling lived on Brownsman Island when she was a child when her father used to be the lighthouse keeper there, but that lighthouse was decommissioned in 1826 the same time Longstone was lit. The Golden Gate boat trip takes you past Brownsman Island and allows you to see the rock where the ship was wrecked and will give you a sense of the distance she and her father had to row in the stormy seas.

You will also get to see some seals. The picture below is a photograph I took on the boat trip to Longstone.

We even got to see a seal pup close up on Longstone Island.

Chester Le Street

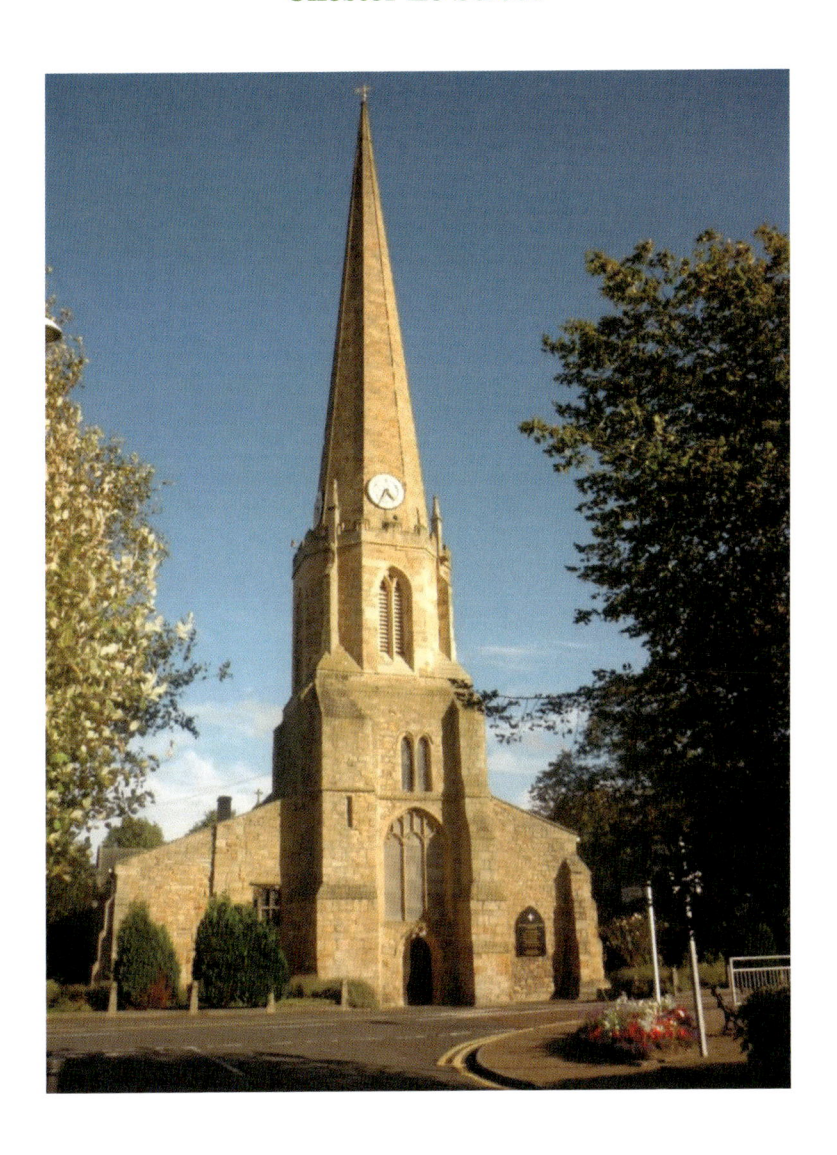

The church of St Mary and St Cuthbert is an interesting place to visit as it was the church where the monks brought the remains of St Cuthbert after the Viking invasion of Lindisfarne, and here they settled for a hundred years before St Cuthbert's remains were finally laid to rest in Durham Cathedral.

Inside the church you will find art work depicting the story of the monks bringing St Cuthbert's wooden coffin to Chester Le Street. The church also has an Anker's house dating back to the 14th century that you can explore. The Parish centre across the road can open up the church and Anker's house for you. *Parish Centre, Church Chare, Chester Le Street, DH3 3QB 0191 3883295*

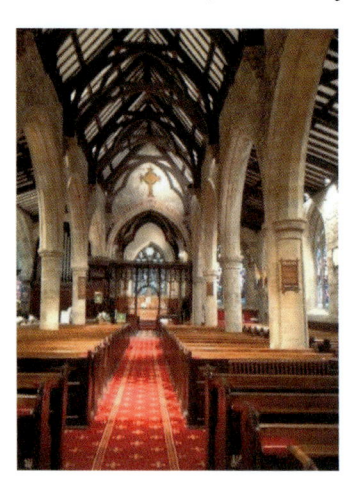

Chester Le Street has roots back to the Roman times when it used to be called <u>Concangis</u> and it is now famous for its international Cricket Ground, Durham County Cricket club 'The Riverside'.

It is popular with young families too as it has an adventure playground near the river.

Lumley Castle, above, is a glamorous hotel and venue for dining and they specialise in weddings. Unfortunately they do not offer tours of the site. But if you book a meal or stay overnight, you will get to see the gorgeous interior.

Raby Castle

Raby Castle was built in the fourteenth century after the Bishop of Durham, Thomas Hatfield allowed John De Neville to fortify his property. The castle and the land surrounding it, needed protecting against The Scots and the Picts and the Nevilles employed a large army of knights to protect it. The Nevilles owned the Castle from 1378 to 1569. Charles Neville fought with Thomas Percy to attempt to get catholic Mary Queen of Scots back on the throne. During 'The Uprising of the North' Queen Elizabeth's army defeated Neville's and Percy's army and retained the castle as their own. Charles Neville fled to the Netherlands where he died in poverty.

In 1626 the castle was sold to Sir Henry Vane, a prominent member of Charles I's household. The Castle remains in this same family today, the current owner being 11th Lord Barnard.

The castle stands in a deer park, and you will not fail to see deer here as you walk up to the castle. They roam around freely and sometimes are around the back of the castle. If you wander onto the grass be careful where you trod.

The castle is open from 1pm and there is a hut at the entrance where you can buy a ticket and a large car park. The cost in July 2014 was £10 for an adult ticket to see inside the castle and gardens. There is a gift shop and tea room built into the old stables. As Lord Barnard still resides in the castle some of the areas are private. It took about an hour to wander around the castle. Be sure to ask the guides in the rooms about the interior, they will gladly reveal the full history to you helping you get more from your visit.

More Books By Sarah Lee

If you have found this book useful please leave a review on Amazon.

Other books by this author.

If you enjoyed this book by Sarah Lee you may enjoy other books by the author.

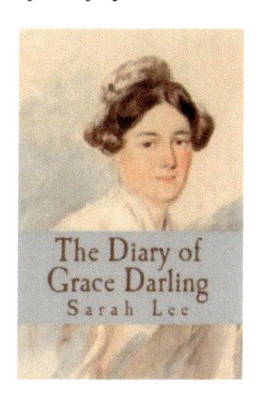

The true story of Grace Darling is a remarkable one. She lived in Longstone Lighthouse on Longstone Island, which is one of the Farne Islands, off the coast of North East England. On 7th September 1838 she spotted a shipwreck against one of the neighbouring rocky Islands. She persuaded her father to go with her to try and rescue the people trapped, and clinging to the rock in dangerous stormy seas. She and her father set off in their small rowing boat, risking their lives, and managed to rescue nine people from the rocks and took them back to safety to the lighthouse, where they needed to remain for a further three days due to the stormy weather. Grace was viewed as a heroine, as such a young woman, only 22 years of age, had great courage and strength, and was awarded gold and silver medals for her bravery.

She died sadly just a few years later, and many a story has been written about her life. This book offers a new perspective, in that it is written in the first person as a diary.

The author has researched her life at length, and wanted to breathe life into the heroine, and view the disaster as how she experienced it and the aftermath of fame she had to deal with.She developed a close relationship with The Duke of Northumberland, and when he saw she was finding it difficult to deal with the fame, offered to be her guardian. So this work of fiction presented in a diary is based on the true story of Grace Darling.

SALZBURG TRAVEL GUIDE

INCLUDES 'SOUND OF MUSIC' LOCATIONS GUIDE

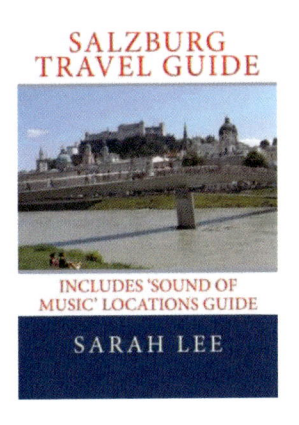

SARAH LEE

New up to date travel guide. Get the most from your holiday with this easy to follow travel guide. This is a simple guide to the most popular attractions including those relating to 'The Sound of Music' and Mozart. It is intended for those wanting to see the highlights of Salzburg and make it easy to find those places and offers some content on the history of the location. I wanted to make it easy to find and locate the places you want to go to so the maps are next to each location in the book to help make it easy for you.

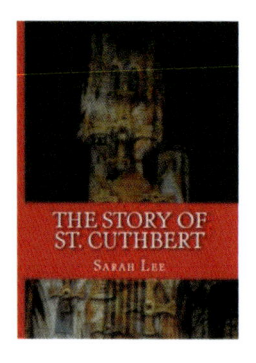

St Cuthbert desired to become a monk as a boy after witnessing St Aidan's spirit being carried into heaven by angels. He became a monk at Melrose, then Prior and Bishop at Lindisfarne. During his lifetime he became famous for his healings and miracles, and even after death miraculous healings at his graveside would take place. His resting place has been a place of pilgrimage for over thirteen hundred years. After the Viking invasion the monks were forced to abandon their priory at Lindisfarne taking St Cuthbert's coffin with them. He now lies in Durham Cathedral. This book is to share with you the story of the most popular saint in Northern England, St Cuthbert.

Addresses of Attractions

Alnwick Castle

Alnwick
Northumberland
NE66 1NQ

Angel of the North

Gateshead,

Tyne and Wear

NE8 7UB

Arbeia Roman Fort & Museum
Baring Street, South Shields,
NE33 2BB

Tel: (0191) 456 1369

Bamburgh Castle,
Bamburgh,
Northumberland,
NE69 7DF

General Enquiries:

+44(0)1668 214515

Barnard Castle

Nr Galgate,

Barnard Castle,

County Durham

DL12 8PR

0870 333 1181

Beamish Museum

County Durham

DH9 0RG

0191 3704000

Bede's World, Church Bank, Jarrow, Tyne & Wear, NE32 3DY

0191 489 2106.

Open seven days a week, closed for part of December and January.

Boat Trips to Farne islands

Billy Shiel's Boat trips is one of the companies offering boat trips to Inner Farne.

NE68 7YT

01665 720308

01665 720316

Golden Gate Boat Trip to Longstone Lighthouse.

 Booking office:

01665 721210

07904800590

NE68 7YT

Daily sailings from April to October depending on the weather. You can buy a ticket from their stalls at North Sunderland Harbour in Seahouses.

Blue Reef Aquarium,

Grand Parade,

Tynemouth,

Tyne & Wear,

NE30 4JF.

Tel 01912581031

The Bowes Museum

Barnard Castle

County Durham

DL12 8NP

01833 690606

China Town

Stowell Street

Newcastle Upon Tyne

NE1 4YB

Durham Cathedral and Castle

Durham, County Durham

DH1 3RN

The Undercroft Restaurant 0191 386 3721

Durham Cathedral Shop 0191 386 8669

Education Centre 0191 386 4266 (Ext 4)

Eldon Square Multi Storey Car Park
Percy Street
Newcastle Upon Tyne
NE1 7RZ
0191 2611891

Finchale Abbey

Durham

DH1 5SH

0191 386 3828

The Gate, Newgate Street,

Newcastle Upon Tyne

NE1 5TG

0191 223 5000

The Grace Darling Museum
Radcliffe Road
Bamburgh
Northumberland
NE69 7AE

Telephone: 01668 214 91

The **High Force** Hotel is just opposite the entrance to the waterfall.

The High Force Hotel
Forest-in-Teesdale
Barnard Castle

01833 622209

Holy Island

TD15 2SE

01289 389244

Laing Art Gallery,

New Bridge Street,

Newcastle Upon Tyne

NE1 8AG

Lumley Castle

Chester le Street,

County Durham DH3 4NX
0191 389 1111

The Marsden Grotto,

Coast Road, South Shields, Tyne and Wear, NE34 7BS

Tel. +44 191 455 6060

Metro Centre

St Michael's Way,

Gateshead.

NE11 9YG.

Newcastle Keep and Black Gate,
Castle Garth,
Newcastle upon Tyne
NE1 1RQ
+44 0191 2327938

Penshaw Monument
Chester Road,Penshaw

DH4 7NJ

01723 870423

Seaton Sluice

Northumberland

NE26 4RD

South Shields
Tyne and Wear
NE33 2LD

St. Mary's Lighthouse
St. Mary's Island
Whitley Bay
Tyne & Wear
NE26 4RS

Tel: 0191 200 8650

Tynemouth Castle

And Priory,

Pier Road,

Tynemouth,

Tyne and Wear - NE30 4BZ

0870 333 1181

Washington Old Hall,

The Avenue,

Washington,

Tyne and Wear.

NE38 7LE

Other places to visit in Newcastle Upon Tyne.

Life Science Centre,

Times Square,

Newcastle upon Tyne, NE1 4EP
Sat Nav reference: NE4 7AD

The Centre for life is an interactive science museum suitable for Adults and children of all ages. Interactive exhibitions vary such as planetariums and dinosaur worlds, and this year they have a 4D ride.

The Discovery Museum.

Discovery Museum
Blandford Square
Newcastle upon Tyne
NE1 4JA
Tel: (0191) 232 6789

The Hancock Museum

Great North Museum: Hancock

Barras Bridge
Newcastle upon Tyne
NE2 4PT

Tel: (0191) 222 6765

Hadrian's Wall
Haydon Bridge
Northumberland
NE47 6NN

+44 01434 344363

Addresses of evening entertainment

In Newcastle Upon Tyne.

Aspers Sports Bar

Stowell Street

Newcastle,

NE1 4XQ

Bambu

Grainger Quarter,
NE1 1UW

Chase Bar

10-15 Sandhill,
Quayside,
NE1 3AF

City Hall

Northumberland Road,

Newcastle Upon Tyne

NE1 8SF

City Vaults

13 - 15 Bigg Market,
Newcastle Upon Tyne,
NE1 1UN

The Cooperage

32 Close,

Quayside

Newcastle Upon Tyne

NE1 3RF

The Gate, Newgate Street,

Newcastle Upon Tyne

NE1 5TG

0191 223 5000

The Hyena Comedy Club

17 Leazes Lane

Newcastle,

Tyne and Wear

NE1 4PF

Jimmyz Bar

8-52 Sandhill,
Quayside,
NE1 3JF

The Lodge

28 Mosley Street,
Newcastle Upon Tyne,
NE1 1DF

O2 Academy Newcastle,
Westgate Road,
NE1 1SW

Picher and Piano

108 Quayside,

Newcastle,

NE1 3DX

Revolution

Collingwood Street,

Newcastle upon Tyne

NE1 1JF

The Riverside Club

1 The Close,
Quayside,
Newcastle,
NE1 3RQ

The Sage
St Mary's Square,
Gateshead Quays,
Gateshead,

NE8 2JR

The Sunderland Empire Theatre

High Street West
Sunderland
Tyne and Wear
SR1 3EX

The Theatre Royal

100 Grey St

Newcastle upon Tyne,

NE1 6BR

Tiger Tiger

The Gate,

Newgate St,

Newcastle,

NE1 5RE

The Waterside Hotel,
48-52 Sandhill,
Quayside,
Newcastle,
NE1 3JF

Printed in Great Britain
by Amazon